D1125283

LeBron James

by John Hareas

SCHOLASTIC INC.
New York Toronto London Auckland Sydney
Mexico City New Delhi Hong Kong Buenos Aires

Dedication: To my new niece, Avyi: Thank you for brightening my world– J.H.

PHOTO CREDITS

All images copyright NBAE/Getty Images Cover: Rocky Widner; (1)Nathaniel S. Butler; (3) Sam Forencich; (4) Nathaniel S. Butler; (10) NBA Photos; (13) Garrett Ellwood; (14) Jesse D. Garrabrant; (16) Nathaniel S. Butler; (17) Jesse D. Garrabrant; (19) David Liam Kyle; (20) Rocky Widner; (21) Nathaniel S. Butler; (25) Nathaniel S. Butler; (26) Tony Morrison; (27) David Liam Kyle; (28) Stuart Hannagan

ISBN 0-439-70397-2

12 11 10 9 8 7 6 5 4 3   6 7 8 9/0

Printed in the U.S.A.
First printing, February 2005
Book Design: Louise Bova

King of the Court

The buildup was great. The hype — through the roof. LeBron James was one of the best known basketball players anywhere *before* he ever set foot on an NBA court. That's what three national high school player-of-the-year honors and three state championships will do. And, when

your high school games are on national television (watched by millions!) and NBA players such as Shaquille O'Neal visit, you know you are a big deal. There isn't any doubt that LeBron is special, both on and off the court.

At 18 years old, LeBron quickly proved why he ranked among the world's greatest basketball players and drew praise from admirers everywhere.

In addition, LeBron helped double the Cleveland Cavaliers' victory total from 17 to 35 games and ranked among the league leaders in points, assists, steals, and field goals. He also became only the third rookie in NBA history to average 20 points, five rebounds, and five assists in a season. The only other two players to accomplish this feat: Oscar Robertson and Michael Jordan — two superstars who went on to win NBA Championships!

So, it wasn't surprising that LeBron won the NBA's top rookie honors, or that he was named to the Men's U.S.A. Senior National Team that competed in the 2004 Summer Olympics in Athens, Greece.

"Regardless of his age, he's a special player," said New Jersey head coach Lawrence Frank after watching LeBron drop 41 points on the Nets in a regular-season game.

And the fans agree. People of all ages wore No. 23 wine-and-gold uniforms everywhere the Cavaliers played. When he made a spectacular move during a road game, the other team's home crowd would cheer — loudly. The Cavaliers quickly became one of the NBA's most popular teams and LeBron's jersey was the No. 1 seller among all current players.

While LeBron dazzled on the court, he remained grounded off of it. Maybe even more impressive than his statistics was the way he handled all of the pressure. He never let it affect him.

Instead, he made sure he had fun playing the game he loves. While his skills are beyond his years, his maturity also scores high marks. Through both winning and losing streaks that

came his way, LeBron always maintained his wonderful smile.

LeBron is also very unselfish. He'll give up a basket for himself to set up a teammate so he can score. He has the ability to make other players around him better. Players such as Robertson, Magic Johnson, Larry Bird, and Jordan — the game's all-time greats — also had that rare gift.

"Where he gets his vision from, I just don't know," says Paul Silas, the Cavaliers' head coach. "He can see passes nobody else can, and they're right on the money."

Most of all, LeBron likes to have fun. Away from the game, he loves to play video games and hang out with his buddies, of whom he has plenty. After all, Cleveland is only 40 miles from where LeBron grew up, in Akron, Ohio. It's important for him to share his success. He not only stays close to his childhood friends and donates his time to local charities, he also enjoys a close relationship with his personal hero, his mom.

Fame hasn't changed LeBron. He's the same person who grew up admiring Michael Jordan. Now, fans are admiring *him*.

Here is his story.

Growing Up

LeBron James was born on December 30, 1984 (exactly nine years to the day after Tiger Woods's birthday!) in Akron, Ohio. Akron was known as the rubber capital of the world. It was home to the world's biggest companies that produced tires for all kinds of vehicles, from horse-drawn carriages to bicycles and cars.

An only child, LeBron was raised by his mom, Gloria. Raising a child as a single parent is challenging and it wasn't any easier for Gloria. Making ends meet often meant instability — living in different apartments and changing schools — throughout LeBron's youth. It was not an easy time, especially since his mom was also looking out for his two uncles.

"My mom is great," said LeBron. "She's the only parent I've ever had. For her to be so strong, to raise a child of her own and her two brothers just shows what a special person she is."

Moving around and changing schools affected young LeBron. He missed 82 days out of 160 in the fourth grade, and it was hard having to make new friends all the time.

LeBron's two favorite sports were basketball and football, and he channeled his frustration onto the football, field. LeBron excelled in peewee football, where he played wide receiver. In his first season, he scored 19 touchdowns in six games!

LeBron became friends with his fourth-grade classmates: Dru Joyce III, Frankie Walker, Willie McGee, and Sian Cotton. They all shared a love of sports, especially basketball.

Frankie's father, Frankie Sr., had heard about LeBron's athletic talent and also that he missed a lot of school. Hoping to get LeBron back on track, he spoke to Gloria about letting LeBron live with his family. She agreed, and LeBron moved in with the Walker family in fifth grade.

It was a life-changing move for LeBron. The family, consisting of three kids — Frankie Jr., Chanelle, and Tanesha — as well as Frankie Sr. and his wife, Pam, provided LeBron with a strong home environment. Homework and chores were required in the Walker household and this discipline helped LeBron to flourish. One year after missing more than half of the school year, LeBron received the attendance award for fifth grade. LeBron moved back with his mom the following year, splitting time with her and the Walker family.

In addition to helping LeBron get back on track at school, Frankie Sr. recognized his talent on the basketball court and helped teach him the fundamentals while emphasizing an all-around game. Soon LeBron and his four friends were playing basketball on an Amateur Athletic Union (AAU) team. "It was great for me having those guys around, especially since I didn't have a brother or sister," said LeBron. "We traveled around to different AAU Tournaments and called ourselves the Fab Five."

Their team, the Northeast Ohio Shooting Stars, participated in the AAU Championships in sixth grade in Salt Lake City and two years later advanced to the finals when they were held in Orlando.

The team's success — they went on to win more than 200 AAU Tournament games — laid the groundwork for future greatness, which was right around the corner.

High School Sensation

By the time he had finished the eighth grade, LeBron was becoming a star with his all-around selfless style of play. He and his friends decided to attend the same high school: St. Vincent-St. Mary in Akron.

St. Vincent-St. Mary rolled to a 27–0 record, winning the Division III state title in the Fab Five's freshman season. LeBron starred for the Irish, averaging 18 points and six rebounds, a game. In the championship game against Greenview (Jamestown), the local hero scored 25 points, pulled down nine rebounds, and dished four assists in his team's 73–55 win.

LeBron's sophomore season featured more great play. He led his team to a 26–1 record and

another Division III title. He averaged 25.2 points, 7.2 rebounds, 5.8 assists, and 3.8 steals for the season. St. Vincent-St. Mary finished fifth in the *USA Today* Super 25 rankings, and LeBron became the first sophomore player ever to be chosen for *USA Today*'s All-USA First Team. He also earned Mr. Basketball honors for the state of Ohio from the Associated Press.

"We just basically came out every game and showcased our talent," said LeBron. "It didn't matter if the opposing team was bigger than us or taller than us. We knew we had the ability to go out and win every night because we played as a team."

LeBron starred on the basketball court, but he also continued to excel on the football field, earning First Team All-State honors as a wide receiver. In his junior season LeBron led the Irish to the football state semifinals, but he broke the index finger on his left hand just prior to the start of the basketball season.

Despite this setback, LeBron led St. Vincent-St. Mary to a 23–4 record, and averaged 29 points, 8.3 rebounds, 5.7 assists, and 3.3 steals during the 2001-02 season. Unlike the previous two seasons, however, St. Vincent-St. Mary didn't win the state championship, falling to Roger Bacon of Cincinnati in the state final.

The phenomenal success of SVSM made news throughout the country. Soon, LeBron had a national following as fans devoted web pages to him, and the national media increased its coverage.

LeBron was being compared to his idol, Michael Jordan, and appeared on the cover of *Sports Illustrated* his junior season. There was even talk that he could be the No. 1 overall pick in the NBA Draft after his third year of high school. NBA rules prevented that, but the word was out: LeBron was destined for future greatness, and everyone wanted to get a look at him.

In order to deal with the overflowing crowds during LeBron's senior season, the school moved the team's home games from the gym to nearby

University of Akron's JAR Arena, which has a seating capacity of 6,000. The games, which were also shown on Pay-Per-View, were instant sellouts as the team continued to dominate. The demand to see LeBron was so great that ESPN televised some of his games to satisfy the overwhelming interest.

And LeBron didn't disappoint. He lived up to the hype, averaging 31.6 points, 9.6 rebounds, 4.6 assists, and 3.4 steals to lead the Irish to a 25–1 record. He also led SVSM to their third state title in four seasons and the high school national championship, selected by *USA Today*. LeBron also picked up his third consecutive Mr. Basketball honor. Overall, LeBron led the Irish to a 101–6 record and three state titles in his four years.

LeBron continued to shine in the postseason All-Star Games, earning MVP honors in the McDonald's High School All-American Game, the EA Sports Roundball Classic, and the Jordan Capital Classic.

Although he had considered several colleges, the opportunity to fulfill his dream of playing in the NBA and help his mom out was too good to pass up. At the end of his senior year, LeBron announced that he would enter the NBA Draft. The question now was would LeBron's success translate to the NBA level?

As the 2003 NBA Draft approached in late June, there wasn't any doubt who the No. 1 pick would be. However, a little more than a month before the draft, there was uncertainty as to

which team would get the lucky bounce of the ping-pong balls in the NBA Draft Lottery needed to secure the rights for the No. 1 over-all pick. Thirteen teams that hadn't advanced to the playoffs were eligible for the lottery and one of those would land the prize, LeBron James.

The Cleveland Cavaliers finished the

2002–03 season with a 17–65 record, tying the Denver Nuggets with the worst mark in the league. It was Cleveland's fifth consecutive losing season. A team that once ranked among the Eastern Conference elite was now struggling to win games and draw fans. The prospect of drafting the local phenom would go a long way in turning the franchise around. The Cavaliers' chances appeared good since their record increased the percentage of receiving the No. 1 pick. Still, for lifelong Cavaliers fans who had had their hearts broken numerous times over the years, the prospect of landing the local hero seemed too good to be true.

When the lottery came down to two teams — Detroit and Cleveland — and the Pistons received the second pick, Cavaliers fans rejoiced, some even dancing in the streets. The most heralded player in the country was staying home to play for the team he had rooted for growing up.

"I'm very excited for the fans of Cleveland," said longtime Cavaliers owner, Gordon Gund. "This is a great day for them and for all of that market, for Akron, for Cleveland, all of northeastern Ohio. I'm tremendously excited about it. It's a big day in Cleveland sports."

It sure was. Minutes after the Cavaliers' good

fortune, the phone was ringing off the hook at their ticket offices as fans wanted to be in on the ground floor of the LeBron era. Soon, No. 23 jerseys were flying off the shelves of retail stores. LeBron hadn't played one minute in the NBA, yet his impact on the team was already huge.

"I think it's going to be great for me and also for my family that they don't have to travel across the country to come watch me play," said LeBron. "And growing up watching the Cavs was great because it was during the [Michael] Jordan era. I think it's going to be great to get to know some teammates. Hopefully, we can get better."

Playing in front of family and friends also pre-

sented LeBron with potentially a lot more distractions. Many wondered how he would handle the demands on and off the court.

"I'm one of the highest publicized players in the country right now, and I haven't even played one game of basketball in the NBA," said LeBron. "I know I'm a marked man, but I just have to go out there and play hard and play strong and help my teammates every night."

Rookie Sensation

The moment had finally arrived. After an off-season filled with speculation about how well LeBron would fare in the NBA, his first official regular-season game was set to tip off on October 29, 2003.

His debut would be on the road, in one of the NBA's loudest arenas. The Cavaliers opened their season against one of the NBA's premier teams, the Sacramento Kings, on national television. Arco Arena is one of the league's most difficult places to play. The Kings' fans attend every home game equipped with homemade signs and cowbells that clang throughout the game. They are some of the NBA's most loyal enthusiasts.

Perhaps no other rookie in NBA history had so much attention focused on his first professional game. Rather than get caught up in the hype, LeBron remained calm and put on one of the most

impressive rookie opening night performances ever.

LeBron dazzled. Playing the point guard position, he scored 25 points, grabbed six rebounds, and dished nine assists. Unfortunately, it wasn't enough as the Cavs lost to the Kings, 106–92.

After the game, LeBron downplayed his performance, preferring to have had the win.

"I think I played well. Not well enough," James

said. The Kings, who had a difficult time slowing the 18-year-old down, were obviously impressed with his play.

"For a guy who's just eighteen, I'm really surprised, in a positive way," Kings center Vlade Divac said. "He's the real deal. He has a chance to be on the same level as Kobe [Bryant]."

As the season unfolded, LeBron continued to make an immediate impact in the stat sheet but unfortunately it was not enough to make a difference in the standings — just yet.

After his first full month in the NBA, LeBron led

all rookies in scoring (17.5) and assists (6.4), and ranked second in rebounding (7.0). He also ranked second in the NBA in minutes played, with 697. Despite the impressive play, the Cavaliers were only 4–13. It was going to take time for LeBron and his new teammates to find the perfect chemistry.

In order to find the right mix, the Cavaliers were involved in a six-player trade in mid-December to surround LeBron with some veteran players. The Cavaliers acquired guard/forwards Eric Williams and Kedrick Brown and center Tony Battie from the Boston Celtics.

As the Cavaliers found their way, LeBron continued to make headlines with his amazing all-around play. In a Christmas day game that featured the Cavaliers and Orlando Magic, LeBron went up against one of the NBA's premier players in Tracy McGrady. The NBA scoring champ scored 41 points to lead the Magic to a thrilling overtime victory, but the legend of LeBron continued to grow as he poured in 34 points.

"He's unbelievable," McGrady said after the game. "If he continues to work hard and stay hungry, it could be ugly. It's scary how good he really could be."

The Cavaliers continued to tinker with their

lineup and acquired point guard Jeff McInnis in late January. With McInnis now starting, LeBron shifted to shooting guard, relieving him of starting point guard duties.

The move immediately paid off. LeBron scored a career-high 38 points versus the Washington Wizards on February 1, and later topped that performance with another career high of 41 versus the New Jersey Nets in late March. In his finest game as a pro, LeBron also dished 13 assists and six rebounds. It was the most points scored by a rookie in franchise history. At 19 years and 87 days old, LeBron became the youngest player in NBA history to score 40 points in a game.

Even though LeBron was now an NBA star, he was still part of the team. Rookies usually help the veterans, whether it is buying breakfast or running errands and LeBron wasn't any different — no matter how good he was.

"LeBron's part of the team and we're not going to do anything that separates him from the team," said Cavaliers President and GM Jim Paxson. "As far as pregame routines, things like carrying the balls to the bus, he's going to have to earn his stripes."

LeBron did earn them and his teammates liked him that much more because of it.

The roster changes, combined with LeBron's amazing all-around play, had the Cavaliers in playoff contention. The team eventually fell short of that goal but it was an amazing season across the board, topped off by LeBron winning got milk? NBA Rookie of the Year honors as he led his team in points, assists, and steals.

Not only did the Cavaliers more than double their win total from 17 to 35, it was also the most wins for the franchise since the 1997–98 season. The Cavaliers enjoyed a 59 percent increase in attendance from the previous season and averaged a franchise high of 18,522 fans per game (home and road).

The team, which had rarely been seen on national television before, was featured 16 times during LeBron's rookie season while local television ratings and merchandise sales increased dramatically. Reporters from more than 20 countries also covered the rookie sensation.

"I think we really had a successful season, not because of my statistics, but just the way the team improved," James said.

LeBron's play also earned him a spot on the USA Men's Basketball Olympic team that would compete in Athens 2004 Summer Games.

It was quite a year for the Akron, Ohio native.

Sky's the Limit

LeBron enjoyed a terrific rookie season. All of his dreams came true. Not only did he achieve his goal of reaching the NBA, he was also able to play for a team close to home. This gave LeBron the opportunity to have family and friends

support him and to make a difference in his community.

"I can't always sign everything or take every picture, but I will always try to give something back to my hometown," said LeBron.

Every Thanksgiving, LeBron and his friends hand out turkeys and bags of groceries to families in need. He also participates in the NBA's Read to Achieve program, stressing the importance of reading to kids of all ages. In addition, he has donated refurbished basketball courts to a local community center.

Being a role model is something that LeBron doesn't take lightly. It's important to LeBron to

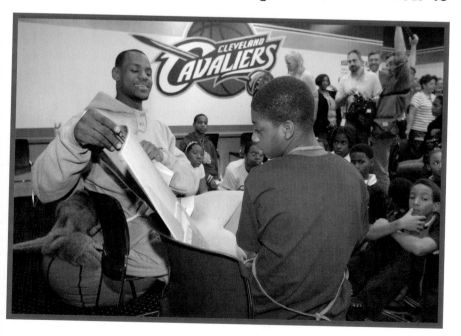

make a difference for young people who admire him.

"I like to help out," said LeBron. "I feel like it's my job to make a difference and put smiles on kids' faces."

LeBron's experience on the USA Basketball team allowed him to see the world. He had traveled outside the United States only once before and that was when he was a member of the AAU team, when he spent two weeks in Italy. During the summer of 2004, LeBron had the opportunity to visit such places as Germany, Serbia and Montenegro, Turkey, and Greece — something he might never have done if not for basketball.

But as big an impact as LeBron has made on the court, he still sees room for improvement. Whether it is working on his outside shot or his defense, LeBron isn't resting on his accomplishments.

It is his tireless work ethic and his winning attitude that will help him to one day become one of the NBA's all-time greats. And it is this commitment to excellence that LeBron says is the key to success, no matter what your dreams are.

"It's about believing in hard work," said LeBron. "I think if you put the hard work into what you want to become and what you want to do that you can be successful. Not everyone can be a professional athlete because God blesses people with athletic ability and the ability to play the game of basketball or football. But if you want to do something off the court like be a nurse, or a teacher or doctor, you have to have a great work ethic and a belief and there is no doubt that you'll succeed."

LeBron has that work ethic, and there is very little doubt that he will succeed in reaching his goals.

READ TO ACHIEVE

Read to Achieve is the NBA's year-round, league-wide initiative that promotes the value of reading and online literacy and encourages families and adults to read regularly with young children. With the support of longtime national partners such as Reading Is Fundamental and Scholastic Inc., the NBA and its teams will create Read to Achieve Reading and Learning Centers throughout North America in an effort to provide access to reading materials and technology to young people everywhere. The NBA has also formed national and local All-Star Reading Teams comprised of current and former NBA, WNBA and NBDL players and other members of the NBA family, who promote the value of reading through in-arena events, public service announcements, and school and community appearances. The NBA, WNBA and NBDL and its teams and players, are committed to developing in children a lifelong love for reading.

For more information, log on to:

READ TO ACHIEVE

LeBron James burst on to the NBA scene in 2003 and quickly established himself as a player to watch. Now he's ready for the new season and ready to prove that he's not a one-year phenom. And you can get in on the action with all the inside facts on this NBA sensation.

READING IS FUN WITH THE NBA!

Design by Louise Bova

ISBN 0-439-70397-2

EAN

9 780439 703970

50399

SCHOLASTIC
www.scholastic.com

$3.99 US
$5.50 CAN

For more basketball fu

NBA
CO

W7-ATG-974